Forward for Freedom: T...

BATTLESHIP
WISCONSIN
(BB-64)

By Amy Waters Yarsinske

THE
DONNING COMPANY
PUBLISHERS

Dedication

This book is dedicated with deepest respect and grati-
tude to all those men who went to sea aboard the
great battleship USS *Wisconsin*, and who when called
upon by their country, dutifully answered the nation's cry
and put themselves in harm's way.

The Donning Company Publishers
184 Business Park Drive, Suite 206
Virginia Beach, VA 23462

Steve Mull, General Manager
B. L. Walton Jr., Project Director
Dawn V. Kofroth, Assistant General Manager
Sally Clarke Davis, Editor
Marshall Rouse McClure, Graphic Designer
John Harrell, Imaging Artist
Scott Rule, Senior Marketing Coordinator
Patricia Peterson, Marketing Coordinator

Library of Congress Cataloging-in-Publication Data

Yarsinske, Amy Waters, 1963–
    Forward for freedom : the story of battleship Wisconsin (BB-64) / by Amy
Waters Yarsinske.
        p. cm.
    ISBN 1-57864-128-4 (pbk. : alk. paper)
    1. Wisconsin (Battleship : BB-64)—History.   I. Title.
VA65.W6 Y37 2001
359.3'252'0973—dc21

                                                                              2001017251

Printed in the United States of America

Acknowledgments

The author wishes to extend her greatest appreciation to the innumerable former crewmen of USS *Wisconsin* who contributed personal archives and photographs to the preparation of this volume, the first of two books to tell the Big Wisky's story. Special thanks goes to Dominic Menta, historian and curator of the USS Wisconsin Association, for his unwavering support and the use of his archives to complete the work, and Edwin J. Feiler Jr., of Savannah, Georgia, for his extraordinary generosity in permitting the use of his photographs. Both of these gentlemen are former crewmen of the *Wisconsin* as were F. Dean Roesler, Robert F. McAlonie, Harold Seavers, John Slanina, Lynn Pickens Barrier, and Jerry Blesch, all of whom contributed invaluable material—and memories—to the story. Then there is Eula Ragsdale, widow of Hugh Clifton Ragsdale Jr., a World War II–era Wisky crewman, who contributed photographs and memories of her husband—the young sailor who always had a Gibson guitar in hand to play for his shipmates when the days grew long and the tension of combat weighed heavily on the minds of *Wisconsin*'s war-weary crew.

The USS Wisconsin Association is to be commended for keeping the memory and spirit of *Wisconsin* alive. Formed in 1988 to promote the history of BB-64 and the camaraderie of all who sailed on her, the association is a vital link for the Big Wisky's former crew.

The author extends sincerest appreciation to Rear Admiral John T. "Jack" Kavanaugh, Supply Corps, United States Navy retired and executive director of the USS Wisconsin Foundation, for his support, as well as that of his Foundation, whose members believe as strongly as Jack that the edification of *Wisconsin*'s storied past serves to draw closer the gap between those who went to sea on the third[1] of the *Iowa*-class sisters and those who have never known a United States Navy with a battleship in its inventory. In the end, the Foundation's mission is to ensure the long-term preservation of the *Wisconsin* as a lasting memorial to those who served aboard Big Wisky and as a tribute to the nation, which built a great ship.

[1] USS *Missouri* (BB–63) was launched January 29, 1944, at the New York Naval Shipyard. She is—by virtue of yard construction schedules—the last battleship. *Missouri*, commissioned on June 11, 1944, was also the last to put to sea.

Into Harm's Way

On a gray, rainy day in April 1944 at Pier 4 in the sprawling Philadelphia Navy Yard, the 45,000-ton USS *Wisconsin* (BB-64) was commissioned into naval service. The commissioning ceremony on April 16 was punctuated by the appearance of several admirals and an address by Rear Admiral M. F. Draemel, commandant of the Fourth Naval District, but due in large measure to the war waging around the globe, the ceremony was low-key for such a great ship. The third of the *Iowa*-class of fast battleships, the *Wisconsin* had been authorized in 1934, years before the outbreak of World War II, and her keel laid in January of 1941. Her launching came two years later, significantly, on December 7, 1943. Three days after she was launched, however, and while she was still at Philadelphia, the Berlin radio said that she had been sunk "in one of the biggest sea battles off Bougainville." Such was the reputation that preceded the *Wisconsin* into battle.

A few more weeks to get ready and the gray nose of the Big Wisky probed her way cautiously through the narrow confines of the Delaware River to sea. Inspections, drills, gunnery, and a handbook of new terms all impressed themselves upon her crew regardless of their time and experience in the Navy—from the moment the *Wisconsin* entered the Chesapeake Bay to its sojourn in West Indian waters, where the swells appeared unbelievably blue, but the days intolerably hot.

After her shakedown cruise, the *Wisconsin* and her crew spirited back to the Philadelphia Navy Yard for a last leave period and to provision with ammunition and

The first battleship *Wisconsin* (BB-9), an *Illinois*-class, was laid down on February 9, 1897, at San Francisco, California, by the Union Iron Works. Launched on November 26 two years later by Elizabeth Stephenson, daughter of Senator Isaac Stephenson, of Marinette, Wisconsin, the first "Big Wisky" was finally commissioned into the fleet on February 4, 1901, with Captain George C. Reiter in command. Almost diminutive by comparison to her successor, the first ship to bear the name was 373 feet, 10.25 inches in length with a breadth of 72 feet, 2.5 inches, and drafted a little under 24 feet. The postcard shown here depicts BB-9 as she appeared in 1906, just prior to her first decommissioning at Puget Sound Navy Yard in November. Recommissioned on April 1, 1908, the battleship ultimately joined the Great White Fleet in July as the battleships of the Atlantic Fleet set out on the transpacific leg of their momentous circumnavigation of the globe, a voyage intended as a reminder to Japan of the power of the United States. (Author's collection.)

stores for the deployment to the Pacific theater. The thought of what lay ahead for the Wisky's crew left lumps in their throats as they contemplated the fierce fighting that made newspaper headlines daily. As the ship departed American waters, one boot remarked that the Panama Canal "must be one hell of a big ditch digging job," the recruit masking his fear by wrapping it in a joke. While the crew of *Wisconsin* had three liberty calls, one each in Panama, San Pedro, and then Hawaii, on the way to action in the Pacific, most of her men were so focused on what was to come that they found the shore leave in exotic ports of call not all that tourist advertisements made them out to be.

Wisconsin's commanding officer from the outset was Captain Earl Everett Stone, a native of Milwaukee, Wisconsin, who was charged with fitting out the battleship for battle. A United States Naval Academy graduate, class of 1918, Stone had been aboard the USS *Cleveland* (C-19) in the first war to end all wars and he was executive officer of the USS *California* (BB-44) when that battleship was damaged in the Japanese attack on Pearl

The original builder's plate of the second battleship *Wisconsin* (BB-64) was cast of bronze salvaged from the whistle of her predecessor—BB-9. (COURTESY OF EDWIN J. FEILER JR.)

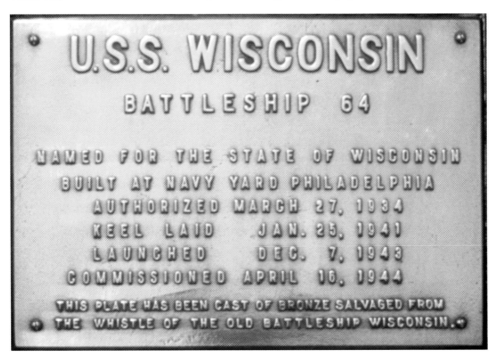

U.S.S. WISCONSIN

BATTLESHIP 64

NAMED FOR THE STATE OF WISCONSIN
BUILT AT NAVY YARD PHILADELPHIA
AUTHORIZED MARCH 27, 1934
KEEL LAID   JAN. 25, 1941
LAUNCHED   DEC. 7, 1943
COMMISSIONED APRIL 16, 1944

THIS PLATE HAS BEEN CAST OF BRONZE SALVAGED FROM THE WHISTLE OF THE OLD BATTLESHIP WISCONSIN.

Rear Admiral A. E. Watson (left), commandant of the Philadelphia Navy Yard, applies the torch to weld the keel section of the new 45,000-ton battleship *Wisconsin* at ceremonies held at the yard on January 1, 1941. Looking on are Joseph A. Schmidt, a Wisconsin legislator, and Colonel Maurice P. Coakley (right), representing Governor Julius P. Heil, of Wisconsin. Heil was governor from 1939 to 1943. Adrienne Coakley Jacobson, daughter of the colonel, was executive secretary to Governor Heil. She submitted the original photograph to the USS Wisconsin Association. (ACME PHOTO. COURTESY OF THE USS WISCONSIN ASSOCIATION.)

Harbor, December 7, 1941. When it came to his new ship and crew, Stone acknowledged the apprehensions of his men but remained steadfastly confident in both the men and the dreadnought he was about to take into combat. The *Wisconsin* reported to the Commander-in-Chief of the Pacific Fleet on October 2, 1944, and dropped anchor off Ulithi, Caroline Islands, to await further instruction. By December 9, the Big Wisky had joined up with Admiral William F. "Bull" Halsey's Third Fleet Carrier Task Force (TF) 38, and just four days later was supporting carrier operations off the Philippines. While the bid to retake the Philippines was well underway by the time *Wisconsin* arrived on station,

The *Wisconsin*'s silver service, a holdover from her predecessor, BB-9, and originally a gift by the state of Wisconsin
to the early dreadnought, was returned, in part, to BB-64 on
the occasion of her recommissioning in 1988. The original
service was crafted in two phases, the first of which
occurred in 1899 when a Milwaukee business, C. Preusser
Jewelry Company on Water Street, was chosen to agent the
actual work to the Gorham Company of Providence, Rhode
Island. The second phase began in 1937 for the commissioning of BB-64. The *Wisconsin* commissioning committee
opted to augment the silver originally made for BB-9, and
thus chose the firm of Alsted-Kasten, established by former
C. Preusser Vice President Charles Kasten, to manage the
contract with Gorham. Gorham made new pieces and refurbished the old. The service was acquired by the aircraft carrier USS *Coral Sea* (CV-43) during the *Wisconsin*'s first
mothball period following World War II, but it was subsequently returned. Once *Wisconsin* moved down to
Pascagoula for modernization, the State Historical Society
of Wisconsin, the silver's curator between stints aboard
ship, dutifully returned a portion of the silver (shown here)
to Captain Jerry Blesch's wardroom. Today, the lion's share
of the ship's silver service is housed in the Wisconsin state
capital at Madison and is used, when appropriate, at state
and university functions. (COURTESY OF EDWIN J. FEILER JR.)

her bombardment of enemy shore facilities was critical to planned amphibious landings on the southwest coast of Mindoro, south of Luzon. With enemy shore installations rendered useless, the door swung open for American forces to attack Japanese shipping lanes through the South China Sea.

While Task Force 38's naval aviators pummeled Japanese air and ground forces from the air, *Wisconsin* bombarded shore targets to make the enemy's defeat more complete. The *Wisconsin* earned her first battle star in the Battle of Leyte Gulf over the December 14 to 16 combat period which eventually led to the retaking of the Philippines from the Japanese. When the going was hot and the air aboard the *Wisconsin* was rife with fear and tension, her crew later observed that the calmest man aboard was the ship's first division commander, Rear Admiral E. W. Hanson, an expert in the deployment of battleships under the toughest combat conditions.

Halsey's sailors had little time to appreciate victory at Leyte Gulf. The ships of Task Force 38, including *Wisconsin*, faced a challenge from Mother Nature that

Wisconsin governor Walter Samuel Goodland (1862–1947) (left) looks on as his wife, the ship's sponsor, christens the BB-64 at her launching ceremony on December 7, 1943. Governor Goodland was a native of Racine, Wisconsin, where he was mayor from 1911 to 1915. He was a delegate to the Republican National Convention from his home state in 1912 and, again, in 1928. Goodland was subsequently elected lieutenant governor of the state, a role he fulfilled well from 1939 through 1943, when he became governor. He died on March 12, 1947. (COURTESY OF DOMINIC MENTA.)

With part of the ship's company lined up on deck, photographer Robert Dumke provided this memorable photograph looking aft on the *Wisconsin* and into two turrets of Big Wisky's mighty sixteen-inch guns as well as some of her lesser batteries during shakedown in 1944. (AUTHOR'S COLLECTION.)

tested the mettle of her men more than mortal combat. One of the worst typhoons ever recorded in the Pacific struck the battle group, catching many ships refueling and with little ballast in their nearly dry bunkers. The storm, which swept through the Philippines on December 18, 1944, was a test of the men of the task force's seamanship ability—and nerves. Three destroyers, the *Hull* (DD-350), *Monaghan* (DD-354), and *Spence* (DD-512), capsized and sank while the *Wisconsin* emerged from the experience with little damage.

While operations off Mindoro were significant to the retaking of the Philippines, the experience was more akin to a baptism of fire for *Wisconsin* and her crew. For the Big Wisky, it would be her participation in the occupation of Luzon and the amphibious assault at Lingayen Gulf that distinguished the battleship. Armed with heavy antiaircraft batteries, *Wisconsin* escorted Halsey's Task Force 38 fast carriers during air strikes against heavily fortified enemy positions at Formosa, Luzon, and the Nansei Shoto, in effect, helping the task force neutralize Japanese forces there and cover the unfolding attack at Lingayen Gulf. *Wisconsin*'s participation in the latter strikes endured from January 3 through 22, 1945, as the ship fought its way into the South China Sea to bait out the enemy's weakening navy. For her support of the Luzon operation, *Wisconsin* earned her second battle star, but the glory of her stars could not be fully appreciated by her crew as they moved closer toward the waters off Japan.

The *Wisconsin*'s first admiral, Rear Admiral E. W. Hanson, made the Big Wisky the flagship of his division upon the battleship's arrival in the Pacific. (Author's collection.)

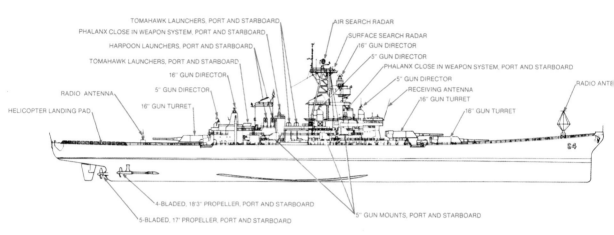

TOMAHAWK LAUNCHERS, PORT AND STARBOARD
PHALANX CLOSE IN WEAPON SYSTEM, PORT AND STARBOARD
HARPOON LAUNCHERS, PORT AND STARBOARD
TOMAHAWK LAUNCHERS, PORT AND STARBOARD
16" GUN DIRECTOR
RADIO ANTENNA
5" GUN DIRECTOR
16" GUN TURRET
HELICOPTER LANDING PAD

AIR SEARCH RADAR
SURFACE SEARCH RADAR
16" GUN DIRECTOR
5" GUN DIRECTOR
PHALANX CLOSE IN WEAPON SYSTEM, PORT AND STARBOARD
5" GUN DIRECTOR
RECEIVING ANTENNA
16" GUN TURRET
16" GUN TURRET
RADIO ANTE

4-BLADED, 18'3" PROPELLER, PORT AND STARBOARD
5-BLADED, 17' PROPELLER, PORT AND STARBOARD
5" GUN MOUNTS, PORT AND STARBOARD

Length: 887′ 3″   **Beam:** 108′ 2″   **Draft:** 37′ 9″
Displacement: 58,000 tons loaded   **Speed:** 33 knots

MAIN PROPULSION
Boilers:
Eight 600 PSI (pounds per square inch) Babcock & Wilcox
Engines:
Four geared Westinghouse turbines
Horsepower:
212,000 SHP (shaft horsepower) for four shafts
Propellers:
Two to five bladed 17′ 5″ (inboard); Two to four bladed 18′ 3″ (outboard)

TANK CAPACITY
2.3 million gallons of fuel oil; 37,000 gallons helicopter fuel; 210,000 gallons
fresh water

ARMOR
Main Belt: 12.1″ tapering to 1.62″
Turrets:
  Face: 17″
  Sides: 9″
  Back: 12″
  Top: 7.25″
  Second Deck: 6″
  Conning Tower: 17.5″

ARMAMENT
Missiles:
  Tomahawk missiles: 32—in 8—quad armored box launchers
  Harpoon missiles: 16—in 4—quad missile racks
Main Gun Battery:
  Nine 16″/50 caliber naval rifles in 3—triple gun turrets
Range: 23 nautical miles
Projectiles: 2,700-pound armor piercing 1,900-pound high explosive (used in the Persian Gulf War)
Powder: 660 pounds nitrocellulose (6—110 pound bags)
Fire Rate: Two rounds per minute per gun
Use: Shore bombardment, anti-surface

REMOTELY PILOTED VEHICLES
  Five Pioneer air vehicles
Length: 14′
Wingspan: 17′
Range: 124 nautical miles
Cruise Speed: 60 knots
Duration: 4.5 hours daylight/ 4 hours night
Cameras: Daylight (Television)/ Night (Infrared)
Mission: Reconnaissance/ surveillance/artillery spotting

SECONDARY GUN BATTERY
  Twelve 5″/38 caliber guns in 6— twin gun mounts
Range: 9 nautical miles
Projectiles: 55 pounds (use varied)
Powder: 30 pounds (in metal powder casing)
Fire Rate: 15 rounds per minute per gun
Use: Antisurface, antiair, shore bombardment

PHALANX CLOSE-IN WEAPON SYSTEM
  Four 20-millimeter Phalanx
Range: 1.5 nautical miles (approximately)
Fire Rate: 3,000 rounds per minute (50 rounds per second)
Use: Close-in air defense against missiles and aircraft

Though *Wisconsin* gained her warfighting reputation with her sixteen-inch guns, the 52,000-ton (displacement loaded) battleship carried a complement of small arms that spoke death, too. Gunner's Mate Third Class (GM3) Donald Johnson, of Hollywood, California, cleans a submachine gun in the *Wisconsin*'s armory, where rifles, pistols, Very pistols, machine guns, and submachine guns were stowed for use by United States Marines attached to the dreadnought. (COURTESY OF F. DEAN ROESLER.)

Facing page: Tugs push the bow of the *Wisconsin* as she prepares to berth at Scotland Bay, Trinidad, during the shakedown cruise in the summer of 1944. (COURTESY OF F. DEAN ROESLER.)

The *Wisconsin*'s first commanding officer, a native of Milwaukee, was Captain (later commodore) Earl E. Stone (left), pictured here with his navigation officer, Commander J. E. Fitzgibbon, going over a chart. (ROBERT DUMKE, PHOTOGRAPHER. AUTHOR'S COLLECTION.)

★★★★★ The Wisky Band posed patiently, sans instruments, on the deck of the ship for their picture to be taken in 1944. The ship's band gave concerts to the crew during morning, noon, and evening meals as battle conditions permitted. Dinner music was typically provided for the entertainment of the officers' wardroom and occasionally in the captain or admiral's cabin. The Wisky Band originated several dozen acts, routines, and feature numbers, besides arrangements and original tunes. A trio composed of snare drum, piccolo, and clarinet played "Bully Beef," a traditional mess call, every evening. The band members' other duties included four cleaning stations, all condition one watches, and acting as pallbearers. The band members in this photograph, two of whom were absent, include (seated, left to right): F. D. Roesler, R. L. Webster, E. J. LeDuc, J. H. Yuill, F. X. Dufault, Chief Musician C. L. Mix, J. M. Coate, W. A. Stewart, J. C. McCoy, R. H. Lambrecht, and J. A. Murdoch. Standing (left to right) are: E. Nemovitz, R. D. Frankel, P. Mina, M. Little, S. R. Mancuso, J. W. Dorrance, J. H. Collins, J. B. Casey, R. C. Rea, R. T. Smith, R. J. Husta, C. R. Willing, and V. W. Schaben. (COURTESY OF F. DEAN ROESLER.)

The Wisky Band, at left, caught in a lighthearted moment, enjoy a laugh with bandleaders Chief Musician C. L. Mix (standing foreground on the left) and Yeoman Third Class (Y3C) Sid Keen (seated foreground). The rest of the band pictured, sometime in late 1944, are (back row, left to right): R. H. Lambrecht, C. R. Willing, J. C. McCoy, R. L. Webster, and R. T. Smith; (middle row, left to right): J. B. Casey, R. C. Rea, J. H. Collins, W. A. Stewart, and S. R. Mancuso; and (front row, left to right) R. D. Frankel, E. Nemovitz, M. Little, J. H. Yuill, J. M. Coate, and R. J. Husta. (COURTESY OF F. DEAN ROESLER.)

Have a Coca-Cola = As you were

...a way to relax on a battleship

Wherever a U. S. battleship may be, the American way of life goes along...in sports, humor, customs and refreshment. So, naturally, Coca-Cola is there, too, met with frequently at the ship's soda fountain. *Have a "Coke"* is a phrase as common aboard a battle-wagon as it is ashore. It's a signal that spells out *We're pals.* From Atlanta to the Seven Seas, Coca-Cola stands for *the pause that refreshes,* — has become the symbol of happy comradeship.

* * *

Since 1886 Coca-Cola has spread around the world. Its refreshing goodness is welcomed by people around the globe. Despite the fact that many bottling plants are cut off in enemy-occupied lands, Coca-Cola is still being bottled in over 35 allied and neutral nations. So our fighting men can still enjoy it many places overseas.

It's natural for popular names to acquire friendly abbreviations. That's why you hear Coca-Cola called "Coke".

-the global high-sign

This Coca-Cola Company advertisement depicts the soda fountain area in the enlisted mess of an American battleship, its ever-popular Coke machine ready to dispense cool refreshment to tired sailors. The ad appeared in 1944 and remains, after more than half-century, a convincing promotion for "the pause that refreshes." (AUTHOR'S COLLECTION.)

To insure *Wisconsin*'s fighting trim, she was equipped with machine shops aboard. Here, Machinist's Mate First Class (MM1c) Gordon Gustafson (left), of Chicago, and Fireman Second Class Robert Remillard, of Sill, Massachusetts, operate a turret table. The picture was taken circa 1944. (COURTESY OF F. DEAN ROESLER.)

The Wisky Band, on liberty in Scotland Bay, Trinidad, in the British West Indies, demonstrated all forms of dress to escape the oppressive heat of the island during July and August of 1944. (COURTESY OF F. DEAN ROESLER.)

Hugh Clifton Ragsdale Jr. was a seaman first class on board USS *Wisconsin* during World War II. "He was always a country boy at heart," wrote his wife. "He was born on the home farm August 7, 1924, and lived there all his life. He was an only child. Until his Navy tour, he was always called Clifton. He taught himself to play the guitar when about ten or eleven years old. Music was a main love throughout his life. He carried his small Gibson guitar all through the war and into Tokyo Bay, then eventually home." Hugh was in the L Division, popularly known as The Lookouts, during his tour of duty aboard *Wisconsin*.

Sleeping quarters were three decks down with no air-conditioning. The men had to learn all the Japanese planes and ships to be able to relay their position when spotted. If the Japanese planes came in, their battle stations were twenty- or forty-millimeter guns. When not on watch, Ragsdale and his division were busy scraping and painting. Benjamin Padgett, a shipmate of Ragsdale, noted of Hugh: "I remember he always had his guitar and could play anything you asked for." Padgett would be the first *Wisconsin* crewman to spot Japanese aircraft on approach to the ship.

After the Japanese surrender, the L Division's crewmen were broken up and given assignments in newly formed divisions. Ragsdale went to the Third Division on November 1, 1945, and there he served as part of the crew of the No. 3 sixteen-inch gun turret. (COURTESY OF EULA RAGSDALE.)

A *Wisconsin* crewman shoots a line over to USS *Gunston Hall* (LSD-5) during a replenishment operation off Luzon in early January of 1945. In early 1945, *Gunston Hall* participated in the initial assault landings at Luzon on January 9, Iwo Jima February 19, and Okinawa April 1. After the first invasion of Okinawa, the Pacific theatre's largest amphibious assault with over 1,200 ships and half a million men participating, the *Gunston Hall* anchored at Kerama Retto, in close proximity, until the first of July to repair small craft. The *Gunston Hall* was not struck by waves of Japanese kamikaze aircraft off Okinawa, though her crew saw several other American ships that were hit and severely damaged by these fierce attacks. (COURTESY OF F. DEAN ROESLER.)

Onward to Tokyo

Assigned to Vice Admiral Raymond A. Spruance's Fifth Fleet (called the Third Fleet when commanded by Halsey), *Wisconsin* moved northward ahead of the re-designated Task Force 58, as the carriers edged closer to Tokyo. *Wisconsin*'s assigned target was a diversionary bombardment of the Japanese home island of Honshu, strategic cover for the invasion of Iwo Jima. As the main task force approached the Japanese mainland under cover of adverse weather conditions on February 16, 1945, Spruance's forces achieved a complete tactical surprise on the enemy. The Japanese lost 322 aircraft, with 177 additional lost on the ground, and took considerable losses both in naval and merchant vessels, aircraft hangars, and installations. *Wisconsin* moved down to support Spruance and the subsequent Marine landing operations on Iwo Jima the following day. Amidst the action, on February 20, 1945, by then Commodore, Stone bade farewell to the ship he had put into commission and turned her over to Captain John Wesley Roper, who directed the Big Wisky in the subsequent assault and occupation of Okinawa and the final strikes against the Japanese home islands. For the *Wisconsin*'s support of the Iwo Jima amphibious campaign, she earned a coveted third battle star.

The *Wisconsin*'s Task Force 58 stood out of Ulithi on March 14, bound for Japan's territorial waters. The resistance was expected to be tough and the mission—to eliminate the Japanese's aircraft threat to American forces positioning themselves off Okinawa—costly. Recognized for her precise bombardment of key enemy

positions as part of Spruance's fast fleet, the *Wisconsin* was awarded a fourth battle star three days later. While the enemy reeled from task force aerial assaults on Kure and Kobe, and on southern Honshu, they were perhaps most surprised by the March 18 and 19 attacks launched one hundred miles southwest of Kyushu, as American pilots struck decisively at Japanese airfields on that island. The *Wisconsin* shot down the first enemy aircraft during Japanese kamikaze attacks on March 18.

The Japanese, however, were not without retaliatory

One of *Wisconsin*'s Vought OS2U Kingfisher scout planes is being loaded on the catapult in this March 27, 1945 photograph. (COURTESY OF THE USS WISCONSIN ASSOCIATION. OFFICIAL UNITED STATES NAVY PHOTOGRAPH.)

"Air Defense—South Pacific," by Dwight Shepler, U. S. Navy Comba

Nerve Systems for Battle Wagons

When a U. S. warship goes into action, officers must make split-second decisions—men must receive their orders instantly. Throughout the battle, orders and reports—coordinating all activities—are flashed by telephone.

The huge battleship *"Wisconsin"* has as many telephones as a city of 10,000 inhabitants. Two separate systems were supplied by Western Electric.

1. *The sound powered telephone system,* with 2200 instruments connecting all battle stations. These battle phones operate on current *generated by the speaker's voice,* so damage to the ship's electrical system cannot interrupt communications.

2. *The battle announcing system,* with 20 transmitter stations and over 300 loudspeakers to broadcast orders in a giant voice.

All this for just *one* battleship! Carriers, cruisers, destroyers, submarines, merchant ships, too, must have telephone equipment.

Skill acquired in years of experience as manufacturer of all kinds of equipment for the Bell Telephone System has been turned to making vast quantities of telephone, radio, radar other specialized apparatus for use on lan sea and in the air. Western Electric is toda nation's largest producer of electronic and munications equipment for war.

To speed Victory, buy War Bonds regularly

75TH ANNIVERSARY
Western Electric
IN PEACE.. SOURCE OF SUPPLY FOR THE BELL SYSTEM
IN WAR.. ARSENAL OF COMMUNICATIONS EQUIPMENT.

A typical battleship, showing some of the important battle telephone stations and units of the battle announcing system. We cannot show all—there are more than 2,

capability. The attack came early the morning of March 19, when a seven-plane enemy formation crept toward the task force, targeting the USS *Franklin* (CV-13), the largest target in the American battle group and the flagship of Rear Admiral Ralph E. Davison, commander of Task Group 58.2 under Spruance. The *Franklin* was then located off Shikoku in close proximity to Kyushu. The first alert was sounded aboard ship at three minutes after seven, notifying the ship's company and aircrews of Japanese aircraft sightings near the task force—and specifically the *Franklin*. Planes were still being launched from the *Franklin*'s decks when watches on the bridge caught their first glimpse of an enemy bomber as it streaked over the flight deck. Two bombs spun down toward the *Franklin* as the aircraft, not fifty feet above

Antiaircraft crews filled the sky around a distant aircraft carrier with a barrage of flak in anticipation of attacking Japanese kamikaze pilots while gunners aboard the *Wisconsin* (foreground) waited their turn during the intense fighting in Okinawa waters in 1945. (COURTESY OF F. DEAN ROESLER.)

Facing page: Dwight Shepler, a United States Navy combat artist, painted the scene titled "Air Defense—South Pacific" for a Western Electric advertisement featuring the USS *Wisconsin* in action in the Pacific. The advertisement notes that the *Wisconsin* had as many telephones as a city of 10,000 inhabitants along with two additional systems supplied by Western Electric: the sound-powered telephone system and the battle announcing system. The sound-powered system, consisting of some 2,200 instruments with connectivity to all battle stations, operated on the current supplied by the speaker's voice. The advantage of the sound-powered system made it immune to the failure should the ship's electrical system be disabled under attack. The battle announcing system, with twenty transmitter stations and over three hundred loudspeakers to broadcast orders in a giant voice, worked efficiently in concert with the sound-powered apparatus. (AUTHOR'S COLLECTION.)

The Badger of April 16, 1945, featured "About the Mighty 'W'" on its back cover. An artist who signed his work "Cornet" drew the sketches of crewmen at work and rest. (AUTHOR'S COLLECTION.)

the deck, pulled up and climbed away. The Japanese pilot was pursued and shot down by Lieutenant (junior grade) Locke Trigg from the USS *Bataan* (CVL-29) after a twenty-mile chase.

The afternoon of the nineteenth of March, task force ships retired from Kyushu to screen the burned and battered *Franklin*. In the process, forty-eight Japanese aircraft were shot down. While the *Franklin* limped back to Hawaii under the protection of a cruiser and two destroyer escorts, the lion's share of the task force participated in the landings on Okinawa. The *Wisconsin* trained her sixteen-inch guns on targets ashore on Okinawa, and together with the other battleships in the task force, pounded Japanese positions and installations to submission and provided key cover fire for Marines fighting their way ashore.

Okinawa would be, when all was said and done, the largest and most complex amphibious operation planned and executed by American forces in the Second World War and *Wisconsin* would come through it unscathed, despite the most fierce onslaught of the war to date of kikusui, the name the Japanese called their kamikazes, which means floating chrysanthemums. Many of the enemy's kikusui pilots died in the hail of antiaircraft fire put up by the *Wisconsin* and her accompanying ships. *Wisconsin* crewmen would reflect later that they had been lucky, but in truth, the Big Wisky's five-inch forty-millimeter and twenty-millimeter guns proved more than a match for enemy pilots desperate to get a

The cartoon strip on the third page of the April 16, 1945, *Badger*, drawn by crewman Walden, gives a thumbnail sketch of the ship's history on its first anniversary. (AUTHOR'S COLLECTION.)

battlewagon. The American task force, however, lost 36 warships and landing craft, and another 368 were damaged. More than 4,900 sailors died and 4,824 sustained wounds, most of which were serious. Kikusui pilots inflicted most of the death and destruction felt by the American fleet during the Okinawa campaign, though the enemy's Baka bombs and explosive motorboats also wreaked a small percentage of the damage.

A typhoon struck the American fleet off Japan on June 4, and though *Wisconsin* once again emerged without damage, three cruisers, two aircraft carriers, and a destroyer were not so fortunate. Four days later offensive operations picked up with a final coup de grace aerial assault on Kyushu. As a result of the action that ensued, a downed pilot off the USS *Shangri-La* (CV-38) was recovered near Kyushu Bay by one of the

The Third Division poses in front of two of the *Wisconsin*'s Vought OS2U Kingfishers in the victory edition of *The Badger*, the ship's monthly newspaper, published September 2, 1945. (AUTHOR'S COLLECTION.)

Wisconsin's Vought OS2U Kingfishers.

With months of intense combat to her credit, the *Wisconsin* eventually put into Leyte Gulf on June 18 for replenishment and repairs. The three-week break went quickly and by the first of July, the Big Wisky and her screen moved out for Japanese territorial waters to support carrier air strikes on mainland targets. Within her first nine days on station, American aviation assets had leveled industrial sites in the Tokyo area and had taken the bombing and strafing campaign to every enemy military target of significance. On the sixteenth of July, the *Wisconsin*, operating again under the command of Admiral Halsey's Third Fleet, opened up on the steel mills and oil refineries at Muroran, Hokkaido, with her main battery of sixteen-inch guns. Two days later, *Wisconsin* pounded industrial facilities in the Hitachi Miro area, located on the coast of Honshu, northeast of Tokyo. The bombardment from *Wisconsin* coupled with that of British battleships of the Eastern Fleet had devastating effect on the Japanese landscape. *Wisconsin* earned her fifth battle star as the result of her operations against Japan near the war's end, but her part in the fight was far from over.

The weeks that followed the *Wisconsin*'s shore bombardment of the Hitachi Miro area saw the task force's aircraft continue to hit Japanese industrial

Vol. II No. 1   **The Badger**   April 16, 1945

Captain John Wesley Roper, U. S. Navy
Second Commanding Officer
U. S. S. WISCONSIN

Captain John Wesley Roper, the seconding commanding officer of *Wisconsin*, dominated the cover of the first-anniversary edition of *The Badger*. Roper, like his predecessor, had ties to the naval intelligence community prior to assuming command from Captain Earl Stone. (AUTHOR'S COLLECTION.)

operations, military targets, and merchant and naval shipping. After the second atomic bomb was dropped on Nagasaki on August 9, the Japanese surrendered on the fifteenth. Formal agreements were signed in a surrender ceremony aboard the USS *Missouri* (BB-63), *Wisconsin's* sister ship, on September 2 in Tokyo Bay. While it may have been a disappointment to the BB-64's captain and crew that the *Wisconsin* was not permitted in Tokyo Bay, purportedly to showcase the *Missouri*, the personal favorite of Missouri native and President of the United States Harry S. Truman, having the *Wisconsin* alongside her sister in Tokyo Bay may have proven more temptation for Japanese saboteurs than the enemy could have stood. Few outside the naval intelligence community were aware at the time that there was a Japanese plan afoot to bomb the *Missouri* as she entered the bay. In fact, the plan was narrowly averted and *Missouri* spared, thus while the decision to preclude the participation of more battleships and aircraft carriers in the events of September 2 may have seemed a snub, the snub may have well saved the day—and countless lives.

Wisconsin ultimately anchored in Tokyo Bay on September 5, 1945, three days after the formal surrender. The ship's crew could be proud of the record of accomplishments (and five battle stars) accumulated in a little over a year in combat. During World War II, *Wisconsin* had steamed 105,831 miles since commissioning, shot down three enemy aircraft and assisted on four more, refueled her screening destroyers on some 250 occasions, received fuel herself forty-four times, provisioned at sea on eight occasions and rearmed at sea four times when circumstances precluded a port call. The *Wisconsin* embarked homeward-bound soldiers and Marines on September 22, having done her duty as part of the occupying force, and departed Okinawa the next day, bound, in the end, for San Francisco, California, after a brief stopover at Pearl Harbor. She arrived on October 15, 1945, to a grateful nation.

While the USS *Missouri* (BB-63) hosted the Japanese surrender in Tokyo Bay on September 2, 1945, the *Wisconsin* was host for a time to 148 Canadian and American fighting men repatriated from Japanese prison camps, an internment which, for most, had lasted upwards of four years. The Canadians *(top picture)*, dug into plates heaped with ham and eggs, while one injured man *(lower left)*, simply makes his way on board the battleship which had earned a reputation as a freedom fighter in more ways than one. The Canadians *(lower right)*, enjoy a cup of American coffee, a beverage they had not tasted in four years of confinement by the Japanese. (AUTHOR'S COLLECTION.)

The *Wisconsin* dis-
patched a contingent of
sailors and Marines to
occupy the Japanese
naval base at Yokosuka in
September following the
formal surrender of
enemy forces aboard the
Missouri. While the Big
Wisky patrolled off
Yokosuka, sailors and
Marines ashore acquired
souvenirs and trophies of
their occupation of the
Japanese homeland.
(AUTHOR'S COLLECTION.)

The USS *Wisconsin*'s softball team posed circa 1945,
perhaps 1946, for this photograph, submitted to the USS
Wisconsin Association by James Janz. (OFFICIAL UNITED
STATES NAVY PHOTOGRAPH.)

"Peaceful" Slumber

After World War II, in January 1946, *Wisconsin* continued to serve the fleet in a training capacity, embarking thousands of midshipmen and naval reservists over the next two years from her new homeport of Norfolk, Virginia. *Wisconsin* spent nearly all of 1947 in this role, and while it was certainly deemed an important service to the fleet, by 1948 the United States had put the war behind it and accepted the euphoria of peace, the kind of "lasting peace" that historically seems to follow great international conflict. The battleships were deemed superfluous and expensive to maintain, outdated in a world without war. With only four years and three months of active service life, the *Wisconsin* was decommissioned and tied up to a pier at Newport News, on July 1, 1948. There she was put in mothballs. Metal covers were lowered over her gun deck mounts and her sixteen-inch guns were plugged and greased to prevent corrosion. Dehumidifying equipment was set up within each of the nine zones of the ship below deck. The humidity was kept below 40 percent at all times. With only a few sailors left to watch over her, the *Wisconsin* had gone to sleep.

Wisconsin's sleep was brief. When sixty thousand North Korean troops poured over the Thirty-eighth Parallel into South Korea in June of 1950, the Big Wisky stirred. As United Nations forces were called to action, the United States Navy moved to recommission its fast battleships. In early 1951 the *Wisconsin* was towed from her slumber at Newport News to a drydock in Norfolk, where men of the naval shipyard reversed the work of two and a half years earlier. Sealed compartments were reopened, guns unplugged, and preservative oils, plastics, and fluids cleaned away. The hull was refurbished and repainted and her four propellers and two rudders scraped and reconditioned. The *Wisconsin* sputtered back to life as demothballing work moved at a feverish pace. "These mothballs don't just roll off the deck," declared precommissioning commanding officer Captain Thomas Burrowes. "And those cocoons the guns are supposed to be sealed in don't come equipped with zippers. And even if they did," he continued, "like all zippers, they would sometimes get stuck." The transformation was rather miraculous—and performed at breakneck speed—because *Wisconsin* was recommissioned on March 3, 1951, with Captain Burrowes in command less than three months after the battleship was nudged from a deep sleep. Speakers at the Big Wisky's recommissioning included familiar faces and important figures from

During the post–World War II years, the *Wisconsin* hosted upwards of 3,400 reserve enlisted men and 390 reserve officers and civilian guests in roughly each five- to six-month period of the year for two-week active-duty training period. There were usually five to six two-week reserve deployments in that time frame. Between January and May of 1947, the battleship completed five Naval Reserve cruises to Panama from New York and Norfolk, steaming a total of over 21,000 miles. The ship could accommodate 85 officers and 900 enlisted men at any one time. A farewell dinner was held at the end of each reserve period in the officers' mess to honor commissioned naval reservists finishing their active-duty training. The dinner held in September 1947 was such an occasion. The menu was provided by Robert F. McAlonie, of Lincroft, New Jersey.

FAREWELL RESERVES

14 To 26 SEPTEMBER 1947

THE UNITED STATES SHIP WISCONSIN

CAPTAIN JOHN M. HIGGINS, U. S. N.
COMMANDING OFFICER

COMMANDER C. K. DUNCAN, U. S. N.
EXECUTIVE OFFICER

U. S. S. WISCONSIN BB-64

SEASON'S GREETINGS

Seaman Apprentice Harold Seavers, assigned to the *Wisconsin*'s Second Division, mailed this Christmas card home to his parents in Peoria, Illinois, on November 12, 1951, during the peak of the Korean Conflict. (COURTESY OF HAROLD SEAVERS.)

the ship's glorious World War II past. Rear Admiral Earl E. Stone, her first commanding officer, praised his former ship from the podium that day in March so many years ago. The sky was slate gray and a cold mist blew over the pier as the whine of sirens and a stream of *Wisconsin*'s blue-clad crew and officers adorned with gold braid and shiny buttons brought the battlewagon to life once more.

Following the customary shakedown cruise the summer after her recommissioning, the battleship remained on training duty until October 25, 1951, when she departed Norfolk bound for the Pacific and the operating zone off the coast of Korea. The only incident that seemed newsworthy during her work-ups did not occur until August 22, 1951, when the *Wisconsin* ran aground in the Hudson River opposite Manhattan as the she came into New York Harbor from Halifax, Nova Scotia. The ship, on a training cruise, was moored fore and aft to floating buoys, but when one of her stern lines snapped, her end swung around and touched bottom off the New Jersey shore. The 45,000-ton *Wisconsin* required the muscle of thirteen tugboats to get off the Hudson's bottom and into midstream. Though undamaged, Captain Burrowes proceeded to Gravesend Bay in Brooklyn to have the Big Wisky's hull checked by Navy divers; there was no damage.

Wisconsin's mishap in the Hudson recalled the grounding in Hampton Roads of the Wisconsin's sister ship, USS Missouri. The Mighty Mo ran her full length on a sand bar between Old Point Comfort and Thimble Shoals Light (the area was subsequently dubbed by mariners as "Mo Flats") on the morning of January 17, 1950, and there she stayed, much of her hull out of the water entirely, for two long weeks. The Navy worked day and night to get the Mighty Mo off the sand bar, but not until her ammunition, much of her stores, her heavy anchors, fuel, and even her anchor chains were unloaded onto barges; not until divers had dug tunnels beneath her flat bottom with hydraulic hoses; not until salvage experts from across the United States proffered their best advice, did the Missouri budge. Wisconsin's grounding in the Hudson seemed altogether minor by comparison to the excruciatingly painful—and embarrassing—plight of the Mighty Mo.

The Marines aboard Wisconsin used Sikorsky HO3S-1 helicopters (shown here in a picture taken from the fantail of the battleship in 1951). The HO3S-1, in addition to the HRP-1, was one of the first two helicopter types used by the Marine Corps. (COURTESY OF HAROLD SEAVERS.)

Conflict in Korea

Upon reaching Yokosuka, Japan, almost a month later, on November 21, 1951, *Wisconsin* relieved the USS *New Jersey* (BB-62) as flagship of Vice Admiral H. M. Martin, commander of the Seventh Fleet. Five days later, with Vice Admiral Martin and Rear Admiral F. P. Denebrink, commander, Service Force Pacific, embarked, the Big Wisky left Japan for Korean waters to support Task Force 77, the fast carrier task force conducting flight operations over select Korean targets. By November, the BB-64 was on the gunline shelling North Korean positions along the coast. During one of her November bombardments, *Wisconsin* was firing her five-inch guns in support of United Nations troops ashore when the unusual—the incident that seems most improbable— occurred. Ground troops called for heavy fire. The *Wisconsin* replied as her No. 2 turret crew swung into action and lobbed five sixteen-inch shells, weighing a ton apiece, into the target area some eight thousand yards away, but the results were rather unexpected. While the shells obliterated two communist-held gun emplacements, the crew of the No. 2 turret had also scratched one T-34 tank. Hitting a tank with a sixteen-inch round from eight thousand yards away is a bit like "potting a mouse with an elephant gun," wrote one observer. "There isn't much left of the mouse."

Though occasionally relieved on the gunline, more often referred to as the "bombline," by a heavy cruiser, *Wisconsin* rendered fire support almost consistently throughout 1951 and into 1952. It was during a fire-support mission on March 15, 1952, in which the *Wisconsin*

Trying to keep warm on the windswept deck of the ship was difficult. Harold Seavers, a young seaman apprentice, did his best to bundle up while not impeding his duties topside. Seavers provided the photograph, taken in the winter of 1951.

A Bell HTL-2 sits aft on the *Wisconsin* during operations off the coast of Korea in 1952. There are two aircrewmen sitting in the "goldfishbowl" cockpit of the HTL-2 as it is refueled. The HTL-2 was first delivered to the fleet in 1949. (COURTESY OF LYNN P. BARRIER.)

Members of his division gave then Lieutenant Commander Elmo R. "Bud" Zumwalt Jr. (standing left center in Navy khakis) a farewell party aboard the *Wisconsin* in June 1952. A dozen years later, Zumwalt would become, at age forty-four, the youngest officer ever promoted to rear admiral. After his command of United States Naval Forces in Vietnam from 1968 to 1970, at age forty-nine, he was appointed Chief of Naval Operations, thus becoming the youngest four-star admiral in Navy history up to that time. (OFFICIAL UNITED STATES NAVY PHOTOGRAPH. PICTURE COURTESY OF JOHN SLANINA AND THE USS WISCONSIN ASSOCIATION.)

trained her guns on North Korean railway transport in the Song-jin area, that the battleship received her first and only direct hit. One of four rounds from a communist 155-millimeter gun battery struck the shield of a starboard forty-millimeter mount. Although little material damage resulted, three of *Wisconsin*'s crew were hurt. The *Wisconsin*'s return broadside obliterated the enemy gun emplacement, prompting an escort ship to signal "Temper, Temper" by its flashing light. She returned to Yokosuka four days later. *Wisconsin* earned a sixth battle star for her service off the Korean coast.

Relieved on April 1, 1952, as flagship of the Seventh Fleet by sister ship *Iowa*, *Wisconsin* left Japan bound for home, but with one important stopover. En route BB-64 stopped over in Guam to take part in the first successful test of the Navy's largest floating drydock, marking the first time that an *Iowa*-class battleship had ever utilized that type of facility. Homeward bound for Norfolk, the *Wisconsin* arrived in early June to resume her role as a training ship, embarking—once again—thousands of midshipmen and reservists, including many of the Navy's future flag officers. This role would continue for a little over five years, but not without some challenges. On

Gun crews on USS *Wisconsin* fired a three-gun salvo from the No. 1 gun turret off the coast of Korea in 1952.
(Courtesy of Lynn Pickens Barrier.)

May 6, 1956, while operating in a heavy fog off the Virginia Capes, *Wisconsin* and the destroyer USS *Eaton* (DDE-510) collided. The destroyer inadvertently cut across *Wisconsin*'s course in response to an emergency search and rescue mission. *Wisconsin*'s bow was cut badly and the *Eaton* was severely damaged. Captain Frederic S. Keeler, Wisky's commanding officer, guided the battleship back to the Norfolk Naval Shipyard for repair. Her unfinished sister ship, *Kentucky* (BB-66), sat at Newport News Shipbuilding and Drydock only 75 percent complete and awaiting disposition by the Navy. A 68-foot, 120-ton segment of *Kentucky*'s bow was removed and barged to *Wisconsin*, a replacement that took only sixteen days to complete. She was once again ready for the sea. For the duration of 1956 and into the following year, the *Wisconsin* continued to train young sailors and hone the skills of her experienced crew. However, *Wisconsin*'s days as part of the active fleet were numbered as her sisters retired from the sea—*Missouri* in 1955, *New Jersey* in 1957, and *Iowa* in February of 1958.

Captain John Odgers Miner was destined to be, however, the last *Wisconsin* commanding officer for the duration of some thirty years. On March 8, 1958, *Wisconsin* was again mothballed, but on this occasion, her absence left the Navy without a battleship on active duty for the first time since 1895. At her decommissioning, one speaker declared the passing of the Big Wisky into the mothball fleet as the end of "the trail for this magnificent breed of ship." Relegated to the mothball fleet at Bayonne, New Jersey, the *Wisconsin* sat idly by without the sailors who gave her memory and life. Eventually she was moved to the Philadelphia Naval Shipyard, where the last battleship—at least by number—remained berthed next to the USS *Iowa*.

Crewmen from the *Wisconsin* went ashore for liberty in Japan in 1952; an all-too-brief respite from patrols off Korea. Lynn P. Barrier, a sailor who spent the duration of his enlistment aboard the battleship, provided the photograph. "It was unusual for someone to stay on the same ship for almost four years," he wrote recently, "however I didn't ask for a transfer nor did they ask me to transfer. It was a good four years and I have fond memories of the experience and the friends whom I met."

Three American warships, the cruiser USS *St. Paul* (CA-73) (background), USS *Wisconsin* (center), and destroyer USS *Buck* (DD-761) (foreground) cruised off Korean waters to make medical and mail transfers. The *St. Paul* had picked up wounded South Korean marines from a New Zealand frigate for transfer to *Wisconsin*, which was headed to port in Japan for replenishment and relaxation for her crew. The *Buck* was delivering the mail to the battleship. The photograph was taken in March 1952. (AUTHOR'S COLLECTION.)

The *Wisconsin* under-
went overhaul at the
Norfolk Naval Shipyard
commencing September
24, 1952. She is shown
here in the drydock.
(COURTESY OF DOMINIC
MENTA.)

The *Wisconsin* relieved her sistership, USS *New Jersey* (BB-62), as flagship of the
Seventh Fleet on October 12, 1953. This photograph, taken the next day of the two battle-
ships tied off side-by-side in the Pacific, was provided by Dominic Menta, former
Wisconsin crewman and historian of the USS Wisconsin Association.

On board *Wisconsin* off the coast of Inchon, Korea, on November 26, 1953, Korean President Dr. Syngman Rhee, flanked by Vice Admiral J. J. "Jocko" Clark and Captain Michael F. D. Flaherty, commanding officer of the Big Wisky, paid a visit to the ship. Accompanying Rhee were members of his military and civilian advisory staff. Flaherty had been in command of the *Wisconsin* a little over two months when the picture was taken. South Korean President Rhee, leader of his country from 1948 to his 1960 spiral from power, was a fanatic anticommunist whose fanaticism led him to kill more Koreans than any other tyrant in that nation's history. While he was democratically elected president of the first Republic of Korea in 1948, Rhee was summarily removed from office a little over a decade later, at which time Rhee and his family had to flee the country. He lived in exile in Honolulu, Hawaii, until his death on July 19, 1965, at the age of ninety. (OFFICIAL UNITED STATES NAVY PHOTOGRAPH. COURTESY OF DOMINIC MENTA AND THE USS WISCONSIN ASSOCIATION.)

The firing practice of *Wisconsin*'s sixteen-inch guns is shown here in 1955. (COURTESY OF EDWIN J. FEILER JR.)

Below: One of the Wisky's forty-millimeter gun crews stands ready for a firing exercise at sea in 1955. (COURTESY OF EDWIN J. FEILER JR.)

The above photograph of a nine-gun salvo from *Wisconsin*'s sixteen-inch barrels, taken on January 19, 1955, during the ship's participation in Operation Springboard, speaks volumes about the awesome firepower of the *Iowa*-class battleships. During her cycle at sea, and including the exercise, *Wisconsin* visited Port-au-Prince, Haiti, in the first months of that year. The picture was provided by Dominic Menta, of the USS Wisconsin Association, who was aboard the battleship from 1952 to 1956.

The Ed Sullivan Show came aboard the USS *Wisconsin* on May 22, 1955. Ed Sullivan (seated in the foreground), the show's host, posed with crewmen on the auspicious occasion of the show's visit. The original photograph was submitted by Boyd Hancock, a crewman aboard the Big Wisky from 1955 to 1958, to the USS Wisconsin Association.

The *Wisconsin* sustained extensive bow damage on May 6, 1956, when she collided with the destroyer USS *Eaton* (DDE-510) in heavy fog. *Wisconsin* was patched but in need of permanent repair. She pulled into Norfolk Naval Shipyard where ship repair personnel removed her damaged section and grafted the 120-ton, 68-foot bow section of the unfinished *Kentucky* to the Wisky in a mere sixteen days. On June 28, the *Wisconsin* was ready to go to sea. (COURTESY OF DOMINIC MENTA.)

The chiefs' quarters of the *Eaton* is shown as it appeared after its collision with the *Wisconsin* in May of 1956. The destroyer's damage was extensive. (COURTESY OF DOMINIC MENTA.)

The forecastle of the *Wisconsin* disappeared under heavy seas during the July 1957 transit from Norfolk to Barcelona, Spain. Embarked with 700 Naval Reserve Officer Training Corps midshipmen from some fifty-two colleges and universities across the United States, she departed Norfolk on the ninth and arrived eleven days later at her European destination. After a short visit, *Wisconsin* headed to ports of call at Greenock and Guantanamo Bay before returning to Norfolk at the end of August. (COURTESY OF EDWIN J. FEILER JR.)

After participating in Atlantic Fleet exercises off the coast of the Carolinas and returning to port on November 8, 1956, the *Wisconsin* entered the Norfolk Naval Shipyard a week later to undergo major repairs. She did not depart the yard until January 2, 1957, about the time this photograph was shot. (COURTESY OF EDWIN J. FEILER JR.)

The ship completed a North Atlantic Treaty Organization (NATO) exercise at Xeros Bay, Turkey, in mid-April 1957, and headed for Naples, Italy, for a week-long visit before beginning exercises in the eastern Mediterranean. During the course of latter operations, *Wisconsin*'s helicopter *(shown here)* rescued a pilot and crewman who survived the crash of an aircraft from the aircraft carrier USS *Forrestal* (CVA-59). The helicopter is a Vertol Aircraft HUP-2. (COURTESY OF EDWIN J. FEILER JR.)

Breaking the two-star flag of Rear Admiral Henry Crommelin, commander of Battleship Division Two, *Wisconsin* served as Crommelin's flagship during the ensuing shore bombardment practices and other exercises held off the isle of Culebra, Puerto Rico, from February 2 through 4, 1957. The *Wisconsin* anchored off Culebra and lowered her liberty boats to send the crew ashore for a taste of island entertainment. (COURTESY OF EDWIN J. FEILER JR.)

Wisconsin departed Norfolk on June 19, 1957, bound for South American waters with a contingent of midshipmen aboard for a training cruise. The ship entered the Panama Canal on June 26 (shown *above*, and *below*) with a deck full of curious future naval officers peering over the side at the girth of Big Wisky slipping through the locks. (COURTESY OF EDWIN J. FEILER JR.)

Right: As she was towed through Gatun Lake, Lieutenant Ed Feiler caught this breathtaking view of *Wisconsin* near the end of the day. A late afternoon sun had already begun to shadow the deck as crew and midshipmen gathered to take in the scenery.

Crossing the Line

The *Wisconsin* crossed the equator on June 27, 1957, sparking a sailor's right of passage known as the shellback ceremony. The "crossing the line" ceremony is an ancient ritual of the sea, but in more recent memory, most sailors can conjure images of King Neptune, his first assistant Davy Jones and Her High Amphitrite. Those who cross the line—and successfully complete the tomfoolery that goes with it—are thereafter known as Sons of Neptune or shellbacks. The night before the ship crosses the line, Davy Jones is welcomed aboard after dark. The ship heaves to and amid much fanfare Davy Jones is hoisted over the bow to deliver his message to the captain and crew. In the picture shown above, Davy Jones, portrayed by one of *Wisconsin*'s senior shellbacks, delivers his message to Captain John Odgers Miner. The following morning, shown at right, the horseplay began under the supervision of His Majesty, Neptunus Rex, and Her Highness Amphitrite. Lieutenant Edwin J. Feiler Jr. is standing to their left in his attire for the day sans shoes.

The *Wisconsin* conducted local operations out of Norfolk from the first part of August and lasting into early September. However, Big Wisky was due to join a NATO exercise that took the battleship across the North Atlantic to the British Isles. During the trip over, there was a show on the fantail with a band and standup comedy routines. (COURTESY OF EDWIN J. FEILER JR.)

Below: Crewmen were holystoning the main deck of the Wisky under the watchful eye of a couple of their boatswain's mates when this picture was taken in 1957. The coarse bricks at the end of each of their handles acted much like sandpaper to smooth and clean the teakwood deck. (COURTESY OF EDWIN J. FEILER JR.)

Below: By the middle of July 1957, *Wisconsin* headed back to the Panama Canal and into the Atlantic for exercises off Guantanamo Bay and Culebra. During her underway period, the sailors shown here were photographed unloading ammunition. (COURTESY OF EDWIN J. FEILER JR.)

Wisconsin's days in the active fleet were numbered as she prepared to make her last cruise. On November 4, 1957, she departed Norfolk with a large group of prominent guests. Upon reaching New York City two days later, the battleship disembarked her guests and, on November 8, headed for Bayonne, New Jersey, to commence pre-inactivation overhaul. The *Wisconsin* is shown here at Pier 7 in New York Harbor on the sixth. (COURTESY OF EDWIN J. FEILER JR.)

Resurrection

Had it not been for a handful of visionary naval strategists in the early 1980s who felt the *Iowa*-class battleships still viable capital ships, the *Wisconsin* might well have remained in inactive status. But what the Navy needed at that time were surface combatants capable of projecting massive amounts of projectiles on land targets, including the capability of firing the newly developed Tomahawk cruise missile. The *Iowa*-class battleships made the preferred platform since each battleship was capable of projecting as much power in one hour as an aircraft carrier could project in a single day, and their armor plate made them virtually impenetrable to single weapon mission kills.

Since *Wisconsin* had been the last battleship of the *Iowa*s to be modernized, she had the benefit of lessons learned refitting her sister ships. She was first towed to the Avondale Shipyard near New Orleans, Louisiana, for hull cleaning and repair on January 2, 1987, then moved to Ingalls Shipbuilding Division of Litton Industries, located in Pascagoula, Mississippi, to begin two months of reactivation work. State-of-the-art Tomahawk and Harpoon missile systems joined her battery of sixteen-inch guns to increase the *Wisconsin*'s striking capability. Phalanx Close-In Weapon Systems replaced dozens of twenty-millimeter and forty-millimeter mounts for close-in air defense. Detection and "soft kill" capabilities, unheard of in her World War II days and only a dream on paper during her stint on active duty in the fifties, materialized in the form of SLQ-32 V3 and less sophisticated chaff launchers. The fifties-era radars surrendered

The *Wisconsin* was decommissioned at Bayonne, New Jersey, on March 8, 1958, at which time she joined the so-called mothball fleet. At the time of her first decommissioning, the *Wisconsin*'s relegation to inactive status left the United States Navy without an active battleship in its warfighting inventory since 1895. The Big Wisky's guns were secured and her divisions assembled as dignitaries and, most importantly, her crew, bid her farewell. (COURTESY OF EDWIN J. FEILER JR.)

Captain Miner addresses the crew and invited guests on his final day in command of the battleship *Wisconsin* in 1958. (COURTESY OF EDWIN J. FEILER JR.)

to the technological advances in radar of the eighties.

Modernization of *Wisconsin*'s propulsion system converted her from the old Bunker C black oil to modern Navy distillate fuel, the same kerosene-type fuel used to power most modern warships. Her 2.5 million gallon fuel capacity gave the Big Wisky the ability to go farther and faster and to refuel the smaller surface combatants in her screen, just as she had done so effectively during World War II. The modernization of her crew berthing spaces would make the *Wisconsin* of yesteryear nearly unrecognizable to her former crewmen. Steel pipes with laced canvas to form a mattress gave way to standard modular bunks. Crew lounges were modernized and made more livable. Air conditioning systems were added and upgraded as the ship neared completion.

The USS *Wisconsin* was recommissioned a third time on October 22, 1988, at Pascagoula, before a crowd of some twelve thousand with Captain Jerry M. Blesch, a native of Fort Thomas, Kentucky, in command. In less time than it would have taken to build a new frigate and for about the same cost, the Navy had the *Wisconsin* back on the gunline. Once again she had awakened from her sleep to roam the seas. Now armed with thirty-two Tomahawk cruise missiles and sixteen Harpoons, the modernized Big Wisky carried more missile strike power than any other surface ship in the fleet until the advent of the retrofitted *Spruance*-class destroyers in the late eighties. With a sixteen-inch gun range of twenty-three miles, 75 percent of the world's population in the littoral land masses was covered by the *Iowa*-class battleships' guns.

The newly decommissioned *Wisconsin* is silhouetted by the sunset of March 8, 1958. While the ship's future appeared bleak, she was subsequently moved to the Philadelphia Naval Shipyard, the place of her birth, where she remained alongside the USS *Iowa* (BB-61) until the early eighties when naval strategists took her out of mothballs for modernization. (COURTESY OF EDWIN J. FEILER JR.)

Desert Storm Victory

With Iraqi President Saddam Hussein's Republican Army forces invasion of neighboring Kuwait on August 2, 1990, a new chapter was about to be written in the annals of modern warfare and the *Iowa*-class battleships would be at the tip of the spear. For the first time since their modernization, the battleships' capabilities and flexibility were tested in modern combat operations. The ramifications of the so-called "test" would weigh heavily on the battleship's future as a warfighting platform.

Five days after Hussein moved occupational forces into Kuwait, on August 7, the *Wisconsin* was ordered out of Norfolk, Virginia, on the 8,500-nautical mile transit to the Persian Gulf. Making twenty-five knots, the *Wisconsin* arrived on station, ready for combat, sixteen days after her departure from Norfolk. Vice Admiral Henry H. Mauz, then commander of United States Naval Forces Central Command, noted that *Wisconsin*'s timely arrival doubled his firepower capability in the Persian Gulf region. The *Wisconsin* was joined almost two months later by the first aircraft carrier to transit from the North Arabian Sea to join her in the Gulf, but for what she had gained in the company of an aircraft carrier, the Wisky had lost in the captain who had breathed life into for the first time in thirty years—Captain Blesch. Blesch had turned over command of the mighty *Wisconsin* to Captain David S. Bill III on September 28, 1990, while the ship was deployed. Though the ceremony was simple—hardly the fanfare of her recommissioning nearly two years before— both men saw what lay ahead for their ship as tensions in the Persian Gulf reached the boiling over point.

A lone Marine stands watch over the brow of the *Wisconsin* on her recommissioning day in 1988. Three of *Wisconsin*'s sixteen-inch guns serve as formidable backdrop to the day's festivities. (COURTESY OF EDWIN J. FEILER JR.)

The importance of doubled firepower would become readily apparent the morning of January 17, 1991, when the *Wisconsin*, acting as Tomahawk Strike Warfare Commander for the Persian Gulf, directed the series of Tomahawk missile strikes that initiated the Gulf War on behalf of coalition forces. Between January 17 and 19, the *Wisconsin* fired a total of twenty-four Tomahawk land attack missiles at strategic targets in Iraq. She continued to serve as the Tomahawk Strike Commander in the Gulf until the end of January when the naval Tomahawk strike package was completed on schedule. Her own Tomahawk missions over, BB-64 assumed the role of antisurface warfare coordinator for the Northern Persian Gulf. She also proved the best platform for a vital logistics and personnel transportation hub. Receiving passengers, mail, and cargo from shore-based logistics facilities, *Wisconsin* greatly reduced the burden on limited Gulf-based logistics helicopters, fondly referred to as the Desert Ducks. During Operation Desert Storm, the Wisky transferred over 40,000 pounds of mail, 140 personnel, and 20,000 pounds of cargo.

When finally relieved on the gunline off Khafji, Saudi Arabia, by her sister ship, USS *Missouri*, on February 6, the *Wisconsin* took the next three days to complete a series of naval gunfire interdiction missions against a

On October 22, 1988, the USS *Wisconsin* was recommissioned for the third time at Ingalls Shipbuilding Division, located in Pascagoula. Before a crowd of 12,000, the Big Wisky was placed in commission with Captain Jerry Blesch in command. (COURTESY OF EDWIN J. FEILER JR.)

variety of Iraqi targets in southern Kuwait. Using her remotely piloted vehicles or RPVs, the *Wisconsin* fired on targets that included imbedded artillery and communications sites, a special forces boat marina, and Iraqi troop concentrations and entrenchments. When the smoke had cleared the last round out of her massive sixteen-inch barrels, the Big Wisky had delivered nearly 120 tons of high-explosive ordnance on target with a high return rate of dead-on hits. For a short respite in the middle of February, the *Wisconsin* returned to the Central Persian Gulf where she rearmed, replenished, refueled and resumed her significant logistics role. Returning to the gunline off Khafji on February 21, BB-64 interdicted Iraqi positions, many located using the RPVs on day and night reconnaissance and surveillance missions. During the following three days, she placed 144 tons of high explosive, sixteen-inch projectiles on target, destroying an Iraqi command and control complex, infantry and artillery positions, and surface-to-air missile sites. When the ground war started on February 24, the *Wisconsin* remained on station in the southern naval gunfire support zone to provide an

The modernization of *Wisconsin* made the ship, once again, one of the most formidable on the high seas. This picture, taken on October 22, 1988, the day of the battleship's recommissioning, depicts the vast improvements made to her armament and defensive systems. New radars and revamped fire control systems were added during the refitting period. (COURTESY OF EDWIN J. FEILER JR.)

As the ship was ordered to "come alive" again, her crew ran up the brows, manned the rails, and mounted the superstructure of BB-64. (Courtesy of Edwin J. Feiler Jr.)

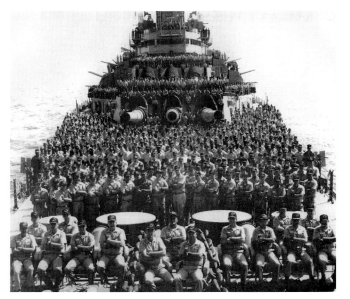

umbrella of sixteen-inch gunfire capability over the coalition forces advancing up the coastal road. As the advance progressed, *Wisconsin* fired twenty-three tons of sixteen-inch ordnance in two call-for-fire missions, quickly suppressing resistance at two Iraqi bunker complexes. An elated Saudi marine commander praised *Wisconsin's* naval gunfire support accuracy because its accuracy had saved his life and that of his men.

As the ground advance moved beyond the range of *Wisconsin's* guns, she repositioned, completing a twenty-hour, overnight transit including a forty-seven-mile-long, 1,000-yard-wide mine-swept channel to relieve *Missouri* in the northern naval gunfire support zone between Kuwait City and Faylaka Island. From the forward part of this region, just eleven miles off the coast of Kuwait and within the Iraqi Silkworm missile envelope, *Wisconsin* fired the last naval gunfire support mission of the war. During this time, the RPVs flew continuous reconnaissance missions in support of coalition ground forces. An RPV over Faylaka Island on March 1, received the first recorded surrender to an unmanned aerial vehicle. Two days later, the RPVs provided reconnaissance and surveillance of surrendering Iraqi forces on Faylaka Island, before and while the Marines took them into custody.

Former *Wisconsin* commanding officer Captain Jerry Blesch (1987–1990) submitted this United States Navy photograph of the BB-64's crew, taken in August of 1990 in the Persian Gulf, to the USS Wisconsin Association. Captain Blesch served as executive assistant for the Commander Naval Sea Systems Command at the time he was selected as the prospective commanding officer (PCO) of the *Wisconsin*. As PCO of *Wisconsin*, Blesch oversaw her refitting for duty at Pascagoula, Mississippi, and became her commanding officer for the second recommissioning on October 22, 1988. He was relieved by Captain David S. Bill III, a Norfolk, Virginia, native, on September 28, 1990. Bill took the *Wisconsin* through the Persian Gulf War.

Fair Winds and Following Seas

The *Wisconsin* was released from duty in Northern Persian Gulf on March 4, 1991, to begin preparations for her return to Norfolk, where she arrived to a hero's welcome on the twenty-eighth. The news a month later must have struck *Wisconsin*'s crew as anticlimactic when on April 29, the Chief of Naval Operations, William Kelso, announced that he was implementing the guidance of the Department of Defense to decommission, prior to the end of fiscal year 1991, the Big Wisky. Through the spring months, the great *Wisconsin* wound down from its eight-month Persian Gulf deployment. The ship made short cruises with former crewmen in what were dubbed "farewell cruises." A new—and last—commanding officer, Captain Coenraad van der Schroeff, took command of BB-64 on April 27. With the annual Fleet Week celebration in New York Harbor occurring in June, the *Wisconsin* got underway for the Big Apple to play host to the Governor of Wisconsin, the Honorable Tommy Thompson, and his guests. Arriving in New York on June 5, the *Wisconsin* led the Parade of Sail past the Statue of Liberty, kicking off the city's festivities. *Wisconsin* returned to Norfolk on June 13 after a two-day transit with more than 150 Navy League representatives from New York and Wisconsin on board.

The last time the *Wisconsin* would be underway as an active-duty member of the fleet was June 14, 1991, for a family day cruise. More than 1,550 family members embarked that day aboard the *Wisconsin*. Three days later, the crew began preparing the Wisky for decommissioning. On September 30, the *Wisconsin* was decommissioned for the third time at the Norfolk Naval Station and subsequently towed to the Philadelphia Naval Shipyard. With the closing of the Philadelphia yard on October 15, 1996, the *Wisconsin* was towed to the Norfolk Naval Shipyard, arriving two days later.

While Norfolk was not the place of her birth, it has become the *Wisconsin*'s permanent resting place. The city of Norfolk, working in concert with the Navy's Mid-Atlantic Command, prepared a permanent site next to

The *Wisconsin* was to play a vital role in the coalition forces' successful defeat of Saddam Hussein's Iraqi forces during the Persian Gulf War. Returning to the gunline off Khafji, Saudi Arabia, on February 21, 1991, *Wisconsin* interdicted Iraqi positions, many located using remotely piloted vehicles sent up around the clock on reconnaissance and surveillance missions. During the ensuing three days, *Wisconsin* placed 144 tons of high-explosive, sixteen-inch projectiles on target, destroying an Iraqi command and control complex, infantry and artillery positions, and surface-to-air missile sites. When the ground war ensued on February 24, the *Wisconsin* remained in the southern naval gunfire support zone to provide a sixteen-inch umbrella over the coalition forces advancing up the coastal road. (AUTHOR'S COLLECTION.)

the National Maritime Center or NAUTICUS in the city's Freemason Harbor area to accommodate one of the four great sisters of the sea. The ship arrived pierside on December 7, 2000, in honor of the day she was launched in 1943, and began accepting visitors to her deck on April 16, 2001, the anniversary of her commissioning in 1944. While *Wisconsin* will surely edify all who step aboard her to the great history of the *Iowa*-class battleships—and of the modern battleships in general—it serves best to remember that it was the fighting spirit of the ship and the respect she garnered from her crew that made *Wisconsin* live and breathe. Better yet that she is left to the memory of the crew who served on her; those men who remember well the Big Wisky's bow cutting through heavy seas at flank speed to reach some troubled corner of the world and the moments that inevitably followed on the gunline with her mighty sixteen-inch barrels firing and hearts pounding, her former crew remembering like it was yesterday the lump in their throats that would not go away and the feeling of fear and anticipation that touched each of them and bound the Wisky's men together in the fraternity of battleship sailors like nothing they had ever experienced before or since. The collective memory of *Wisconsin*'s former crew—the legacy of this great ship—lives on in the memorial ship that has now found a permanent home in the bosom of the Navy. Fair winds and following seas to USS *Wisconsin* and all who sailed on her.

Facing page: The *Wisconsin* returned to her homeport of Norfolk, Virginia, from duty in the Persian Gulf on March 28, 1991, where throngs of well-wishers welcomed her home from war. Despite the sadness felt by her crew after being notified the ship would be decommissioned a third time at the end of the 1991 fiscal year, *Wisconsin* supported a farewell cruise in anticipation of her final demise. The ship also led the Parade of Sail past the Statue of Liberty into New York Harbor in June, kicking off one of that city's most revered annual celebrations. During her Big Apple hiatus, *Wisconsin* greeted some 25,000 guests and major networks filmed their morning programming from her teak decks. Despite the attention drawn to *Wisconsin* after the war, her days on the sea were numbered. This final, silhouetted view of the great *Wisconsin* at dusk was one of the last photographs taken of her before decommissioning. (AUTHOR'S COLLECTION.)

From the workshops, from the foundries and the mills,
Out of the earth and from the minds of men
Came the ship; born of the myriad skills
That mark the age—which in their use condemn
Past forms stagnant and outworn.
A thing of steel, colossus built to lend
The sense of power; created to perform
The mighty feats of Ares' ancient theme.
A weapon forged from strong beliefs, and sworn
To seek out, to destroy, and thus redeem
The heritage of a land inviolate and free.
From the factories and the mines and roaring machines
The product of man's knowledge came to be.

Sleek hull slipping through a white-capped sea;
Creature alive, commissioned now and named,
Tasting tossed salt spray that hence would be
The symbol of her running unrestrained.
Men watched her moods and learned her temperament,
Saw pride born, reviewed her strength ordained;
Saw her guns reach out and scar the firmament—
Then felt her shake Impatience's binding trace
Which curbed her craving for accomplishment.
New men, new ship—each trying to efface
The rub that 'men have made a ship'; none denied
The ship had molded men at rapid pace,
For the ship and men are one, and strongly tied.

Signed "HRG"
From the April 16, 1945 edition of
The Badger

About the Author

Amy Waters Yarsinske, a Hampton Roads native, received her bachelor of arts degrees in economics and English from Randolph-Macon Woman's College and master of planning degree from the University of Virginia School of Architecture. She is a well-known and respected author and journalist, whose publishing interests run the gamut of regional and national history, historical biography, military and aviation history, and nonfiction subject mat-

ter. Though her professional and community affiliations are extensive, Amy is a past president of the Norfolk Historical Society and the Norfolk Historical Foundation, a member of the Rotary Club of Norfolk, the Association of Naval Aviation and its Hampton Roads Squadron, the Naval Order of the United States and the organization's Hampton Roads Commandery, the USS Wisconsin Association, the Admirals Club of the USS Wisconsin Foundation, and a 1998 alumnus of the prestigious CIVIC Leadership Institute. She is a member of Washington Independent Writers, the Authors Guild, and a recent inductee into the Virginia Center for the Book's distinguished Virginia Authors Room. She is the author of many books, among them, *From Hellcats to Tomcats—and the Sting of the Hornet: The History of Naval Air Station Oceana* (Hallmark Publishing, 2001); "Memories and Memorials" in *Naval Aviation* (Hugh Lauter Levin Associates, 2001), *The Jamestown Exposition: American Imperialism on Parade, Volumes I and II* (Arcadia, 1999), and *Wings of Valor, Wings of Gold: An Illustrated History of U.S. Naval Aviation* (Flying Machines Press, 1998). She and her husband, Raymond, reside in Norfolk with their three children.